The Last Supper

Original Spanish version by Mada Carreño
Illustrator: Bety Fischman

Bible Stories for Children

NOVALIS

It was the first day of Passover. Families and friends were getting together to celebrate this special feast. Jesus and his disciples got together just a little before sunset in a room lent to them by a man who lived in Jerusalem.

3

They sat around a low table on mats and cushions. For dinner they ate roast lamb, thin bread and bitter herbs. They had wine to drink and a dry dessert made of nuts and fruit.

6

While they were eating, Jesus raised his voice and said,

"One of you who is eating with me right now will betray me."

This made the disciples jump up in surprise. One after another they asked, "Is it me, Master? Surely you don't mean me."

When Judas asked "Is it me?" Jesus replied, "You already know the answer. Go quickly and do what you have to do." Judas immediately left the room.

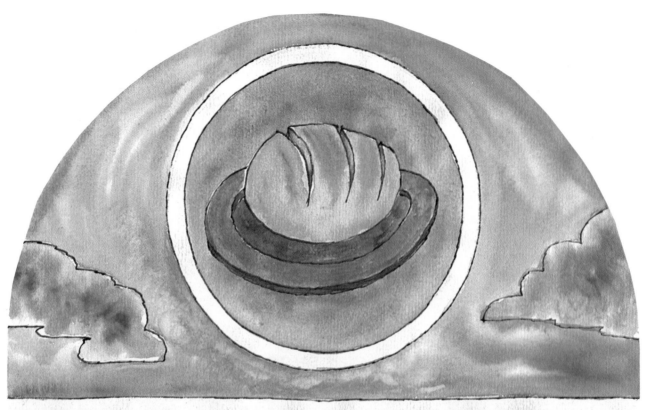

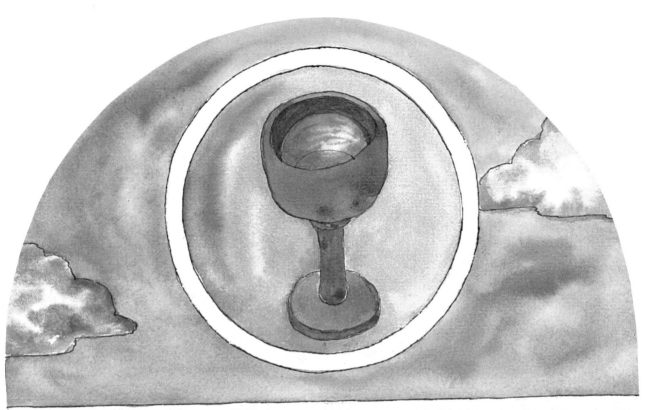

Then Jesus took some bread, gave it to his disciples and said, "This is my body. Eat this as a way of remembering me."

He took a cup full of wine and he gave it to his friends, saying, "This is my blood. Share it with each other as a way of remembering me."

Then he said, "My friends, I won't be with you for much longer. I pray that you will love one another just as I have loved you."

After their meal they all went to the Garden of Gethsemane. While the apostles slept, Jesus prayed. The moon shone brightly.

After awhile, Judas and some Roman soldiers came to the Garden and went to Jesus.

"Hello, Master," said Judas, and he kissed him.

That was the signal. The soldiers grabbed Jesus and took him to Caiphas, the high priest. There they accused Jesus of telling lies and saying bad things about God. They condemned Jesus to death.

Then the soldiers took Jesus to the Roman governor. His name was Pontius Pilate. Even though Pilate felt Jesus was innocent, he didn't save him. The soldiers whipped Jesus, put a crown of thorns on his head, and led him away to be crucified.

All along the road that led to Calvary, a group of women and his apostles followed Jesus, crying.

Once they got to Calvary, the soldiers stripped Jesus of his clothes and nailed him to a cross between two robbers who had also been condemned to die.

Then Jesus said, "Forgive them, Father; they don't really know what they are doing."

Then he lowered his head and died. Although it was only three o'clock in the afternoon, it was already dark. Mary, the other women and the apostles took Jesus' body down from the cross, wrapped it in a white sheet and placed it in a tomb in a cave.

Three days later the women went to the cave, but they couldn't find Jesus' body. Instead they saw a young man dressed in a white tunic. He said, "Why are you looking among the dead for someone who is alive? Jesus of Nazareth has risen. Go and tell his disciples."

The women ran off joyfully to spread the good news.